MW00474597

Every Knee Shall Bow

A Christmas Play
In A Worship Setting

Diane L. Gibson

CSS Publishing Company, Inc., Lima, Ohio

EVERY KNEE SHALL BOW

Reprinted 2002

Copyright © 1999 by
CSS Publishing Company, Inc.
Lima, Ohio

The original purchaser may photocopy material in this publication for use as it was intended (i.e. worship material for worship use; educational material for classroom use; dramatic material for staging or production). No additional permission is required from the publisher for such copying by the original purchaser only. Inquiries should be addressed to: Permissions, CSS Publishing Company, Inc., P.O. Box 4503, Lima, Ohio 45802-4503.

Scripture quotations are from the *Holy Bible, New International Version.* Copyright © 1973, 1978, 1984 International Bible Society. Used by permission of Zondervan Bible Publishers. All rights reserved.

For more information about CSS Publishing Company resources, visit our website at www.csspub.com or e-mail us at custserv@csspub.com or call (800) 241-4056.

ISBN 0-7880-1518-4   PRINTED IN U.S.A.

*To my husband, Jerry, for his
support and encouragement*

Preface

No matter what the stage of our spiritual walk, God always knows our hearts, and he desires to speak to us in our need. Come and hear his words of love, mercy, direction, and promise. I pray you may be so moved as to kneel before him in worship and praise.

The songs and hymns used in this service come from a wide variety of sources. The user should feel free to substitute any other hymns or songs that may be more familiar or suitable to your congregation or group.

EVERY KNEE SHALL BOW

Words and Music by Diane L. Gibson

Refrain: Ev'ry knee shall bow, Echo: (Ev'-ry knee shall bow.)

Ev'-ry tongue con-fess, Echo: (Ev'-ry tongue con-fess,) He is

Lord, He is Lord. Ev'-ry knee shall bow,

Echo: (Ev'-ry knee shall bow) Ev'ry tongue con-fess,

Echo: (Ev'-ry tongue con-fess) He is Lord, He is Lord

Fine

v.1 He was
v.2 He is

born to be the Savior of all na - tions. He was
worth — y of all our — praises —— He is

born to be the Lord of all the earth. (Refrain)
worth —— y of all — our — love

Every Knee Shall Bow

Ev'ry knee shall bow
(Ev'ry knee shall bow)
Ev'ry tongue confess
(Ev'ry tongue confess)
He is Lord. He is Lord.

Ev'ry knee shall bow
(Ev'ry knee shall bow)
Ev'ry tongue confess
(Ev'ry tongue confess)
He is Lord. He is Lord.

1. He was born to be the Savior of all nations.
   He was born to be the Lord of all the earth.
   (Refrain)

2. He is worthy of all our praises.
   He is worthy of all our love.
   (Refrain)

Every Knee Shall Bow

Setting
The Nativity display in a town square

Props
Handbells, heaven backdrop, manger and baby, advertisement signs (one mounted next to manger and others posted around the sanctuary or auditorium), kneeler, tool box (Mr. Charles), cellular phone (Mr. Executive), electric guitar (Rock Singer), crutches (Football Player)

Costumes
Work overalls, hat (Mr. Charles), suit and tie (Mr. Executive), jeans, t-shirt, vest (Rock Singer), football jersey, two angel costumes

Characters

Angel 1	Rock Singer
Angel 2	Sarah (a young girl)
Voice of God	Mother
Mr. Charles	Child (daughter)
Mr. Executive	Football Player
Mr. Jones	Young Boy
Mrs. Jones	Passersby (3)
Tommy	Mr. Good Man
Alice	

God is never seen throughout the play. His voice is only heard as he speaks from behind the heaven backdrop.

Preliminary Music

Opening Hymn: "Oh, Come, All Ye Faithful"

Invocation

Responsive Reading

Leader:	We have seen and testify that the Father has sent his Son to be the Savior of the world.
Congregation:	**If anyone acknowledges that Jesus is the Son of God, God lives in him and he in God.**[1]
Leader:	Jesus humbled himself and became obedient to death.
Congregation:	**Even death on a cross!**
Leader:	Therefore God exalted him to the highest place.
Congregation:	**And gave him the name that is above every name.**
Leader:	That at the name of Jesus every knee should bow, in heaven and on earth and under the earth,
Congregation:	**And every tongue confess that Jesus Christ is Lord, to the glory of God the Father.**[2]

The Message

The Offering

The Prayers

Song: "Come On, Ring Those Bells"

Scene I — *Come and Worship*

Angel 1: *(To another angel)* Did you see what's happening in town this year? They set up a manger in the center of the town square and are encouraging everyone to come and worship Jesus over the Christmas season.

Angel 2: Do you really think people will come? Last year Santa Claus was in the center of town square. People always come to see him.

Angel 1: Well, there are signs up all over town inviting everyone to come. People from different churches are also ringing bells and encouraging those who pass by to come and worship.

Angel 2: Oh, if the people could only know who Jesus really is — they'd see how much he loves them.

Angel 1: Yes, there really would be peace on earth if they would let him into their hearts as their Savior and Lord.

Angel 2: They would see that his gifts are far greater than anything money can buy.

Voice of God: You have spoken well, my angels. Now listen, for I have an important job for you this season. Many people will pass through the square this Christmas. Many will be in a hurry and will be reluctant to stop at my manger. I want you to lead them to the manger and guide them to kneel before me.

Angel 1: Yes, Lord, we will.

Angel 2: But whom shall we lead? There are so many.

Voice of God: Yes, there are many. I will show you who to lead as they come through the square.

11

Song: "Every Knee Shall Bow"

Scene II — *The Groundskeeper*

Voice of God: Let us begin with Mr. Charles, the town grounds-keeper. I want to talk with him.

(Bells play as a summons to come. Angels surround Mr. Charles and lead him to the manger.)

Mr. Charles: I sure am glad the town board voted to allow the manger to be set up this year. It seems like it's been years since we've had it as the center of the square. *(Pauses as he looks around)* It looks like everything's in place — the manger, the baby, some lights, a little kneeler — and all the signs encouraging everyone to come and worship. Although I think people are in too big of a hurry to stop and worship.

Voice of God: Mr. Charles ... come and kneel before me. I want to talk with you.

Mr. Charles: *(Peers closely at the sign beside the manger and begins to read)* Let's see now, "Take time to pause at the manger and worship." *(Removes hat as he slowly kneels)* Stop and wor-ship, eh. You know, this is quite unique. Lots of towns have nativ-ity scenes. But stopping to worship — well, that's another matter. You know, Lord, I'm not real good at words, and, well, I'm not even sure what I should say. All I know is that I've known you since I was a kid. And I know you came to save us and everyone else in this crazy world. Nobody really deserves your love, but you love us just the same. And well — I just want to say thanks, Lord, and uh — Merry Christmas!

Voice of God: Mr. Charles, you have a special place in my heart. I am pleased to hear your words of love for me. Blessed are you for keeping my ways. You cannot even imagine the wonderful things

I have ready for those who love me. Go in peace; I will be with you always.

Mr. Charles: *(As though coming out of a trance)* Boy, I don't know what it was, but that was wonderful! It was as if the Lord himself was right here talking to me. I felt such wonderful love! There just might be something to this worshiping business. I'll have to come back here again and encourage others to come, too.

Song: "Come, Your Hearts And Voices Raising"

Scene III — *Mr. Executive*

Voice of God: There's Mr. Executive speeding by. Slow him down and draw him to me. *(Angels hover around Mr. Executive, who is busy talking on his cellular phone)*

Mr. Executive: Oh, man! This is too much! If one more associate messes up, this whole deal is going to fall through. I need a break. I think I'll take a short walk around the square. *(Angels lead him to the center square as bells ring in the distance. Mr. Executive peers more closely at sign by the manger)* "Pause and worship ... kneel ..." Well, God, I don't know if I'll worship, but I do have a few things I'd like to say to you. You know, every year I hear the songs, "Peace on earth, good will to men," and all that, but, well — I just don't see it. If you ask me, this world is just getting worse all the time. It's a rat race. People are dishonest, they'll stab you in the back to make themselves look good ... Oh, I don't even want to talk about it — it just makes me angry.

Voice of God: Yes, I know all about the mess, Mr. Executive. And it's because of sin that the world is in such a mess. That's why I sent Jesus — to save the world of all its sin and grief.

Mr. Executive: But I don't get it. Nothing's changed. In fact, things are getting worse.

Voice of God: Look hard at the baby in the manger, Mr. Executive. It is this baby that won the victory over sin. His death forgave every sin, once and for all.

Mr. Executive: So then why is the world still in such a mess?

Voice of God: Millions have not accepted my gift and the new life Jesus came to bring. They have pushed aside the very thing that can change their hearts and the course of the entire universe.

Mr. Executive: Well, if you're God, why don't you just make everyone believe?

Voice of God: I will not force obedience on anyone. I offer the gift of faith in the heart of anyone who would accept me. I offer myself to you right now, Mr. Executive. Will you accept my love for you?

Mr. Executive: I don't know. I'm not sure what I believe. I want to accept you, but I'm not sure what's holding me back.

Voice of God: I can change your life if you allow me into your heart. It won't change all those around you, but it will do miracles for your own life.

Mr. Executive: Oh, God, I want to believe you. Help me to believe! *(He buries his face in prayer)*

Song: "We've Got A Brand New Song To Sing"

Scene IV — *The Christian Family*

Voice of God: Here comes the Jones family. Draw them all to me. *(Angels gather the family together as bells ring)*

Mr. Jones: Come on, everyone. We all agreed to come do this. *(They all gather around the manger)*

Tommy: How come they don't have Santa Claus here this year?

Alice: Yes, this is really different.

Mrs. Jones: I think it's a wonderful idea.

Tommy: It's just a manger with a doll in it.

Mr. Jones: Well, the idea is to take time and worship Jesus. Let's all kneel down together.

Alice: I feel kind of strange. Now what should we do?

Mrs. Jones: Well, when you worship you tell God how much you love him and thank him for who he is and for what he has done. It could be a prayer or a song, or something like that.

Tommy: But there are a lot of people around here. I'm kind of embarrassed to do this in front of everybody.

Voice of God: You are the light of the world. Let your light so shine before men that they may see your good works and glorify me.[3]

Mrs. Jones: We can be proud to know Jesus and what he has done for us. Let's sing a simple song and then close in a prayer.

Alice: Well ... okay.

Together they sing:
> Joy to the world, the Lord is come,
> Let earth receive her King.
> Let every heart prepare him room
> And heav'n and nature sing,

And heav'n and nature sing,
And heav'n and heav'n and nature sing.

Mr. Jones: Oh, Lord, thank you for coming for us. It is because of you that our sins are forgiven and we have eternal life.

Tommy: Dear Jesus, thank you for coming for me. I wish everyone in the world knew about you, because you love everybody.

Alice: Dear Jesus, thank you for coming and dying for my sins. I know you are with us all the time and will always take care of us. I love you, Lord.

Mrs. Jones: Oh, Lord, help us always to keep you close in our hearts, to love you more each day, and to share the light of your love wherever we go. In Jesus' name. Amen.

Voice of God: Fight on for me, dear family. Stand firmly in the truth of the eternal life I have given you, and continue to confess my name boldly before others. I love you, too, and will fill your home with many blessings. Go in my peace.

Song: "Christmas News"

Scene V — *The Rock Singer*

Voice of God: Here comes the singer. I've been working on him for a long time. Lead him to my manger. *(Angels try to lead him and at the same time avoid being hit by his swinging guitar and wild movements)*

Rock Singer: *(Comes in singing and rocking with guitar)* Hey, what's this? Is this all the better our town could do for Christmas? What gives? Who was the turkey who came up with this idea? *(Leans over to read small sign by the manger)* Kneel and worship? Hah! Not me! You'll never catch me kneeling before

16

anyone! Jesus is for wimps and nobodies. I got where I am today because of me alone, thank you very much!

Voice of God: Woe to you, oh man of the world. Turn away from all your offenses; then sin will not be your downfall. Rid yourself of all the offenses you have committed and get a new heart and a new spirit. I do not want anyone to perish, but I want all to come to repentance. Repent and live![4]

Song: "On Jordan's Bank The Baptist's Cry"

Scene VI — *The Child*

Voice of God: Do you see that young girl standing in the distance? She has such childlike trust that is an example to many. Lead her to my manger. *(Angels surround young girl, leading her to the manger)*

Sarah: Hello, Jesus. I love you. I'm so glad you came at Christmas. You love everybody so much. You are my best friend. Even when I'm very bad I know you still love me and died for my sins. Someday I'm going to be with you in heaven. I can't wait. It will be the best place of all and we'll be so happy. Merry Christmas, Jesus.

Voice of God: You are precious to me, Sarah. I will be with you all the days of your life. You will see much sin and sorrow all around you as you grow up. But always remember that I am holding you in my arms and will protect you. I will bless all your days and one day will bring you safely home to me in heaven. I can hardly wait, too. It will be wonderful.

Song: "Christmas Bells"

Scene VII — *The Broken Family*

Voice of God: Do you see that woman and child sitting over there on the bench? They have been so unhappy. Draw them unto me. *(Angels bring a mother and child to the manger)*

Mother: *(Buries her face in her hands)*

Child: Mom, it's going to be okay!

Mother: Somehow I feel so far away from God and everyone this year. Oh, I didn't know life could hurt so much.

Child: Mom, please stop. It's Christmas. We should be happy.

Mother: Oh, I know, honey. It's just so hard. Sometimes I wonder what's the point in life. I never thought I would be among the divorced.

Child: I know it's been hard, Mom, but God will help us. I know he will!

Mother: I'm so glad I have you. *(She wraps her arm around her daughter's shoulder)*

Voice of God: *(Lovingly)* I hear your every cry and have seen every tear you have shed. Oh, my heart grieves with you in your pain. *(Pauses)* Look in the manger, my children. Look at my Son, Jesus. If I could give up even my own Son for you, don't you see that I will surely give you everything else? It was for your very tears that I sent Jesus. He brings forgiveness, new life, and hope. Cling to me and my promises. Bring me every trouble and heartache and I will hear and answer.

Mother: Oh, Lord, we need you. Help us to hope again and see the joy in living.

Child: Thank you, Lord. I know you are with us.

Voice of God: Be still and know that I am God.[5] So do not fear, for I am with you; do not be dismayed, for I am your God. I will strengthen you and help you: I will hold you with my righteous right hand.[6]

Song: "When He Came"

Scene VIII — *The Football Player*

Voice of God: Do you see who is coming now, my angels?

Angel 1: Why, yes, it's that famous football player who was injured.

Angel 2: Do you want us to guide him to the manger?

Voice of God: Yes, we shall have a good chat. *(Angels lead the football player to the manger as he comes in on crutches)*

Football Player: Kneel at the manger? Yes, I can kneel all right since I can't stand on my own two feet anymore! What a joke! One minute I was on top of the world, and next — well, look at me now — a cripple! I will never play football again! Do you hear me, God? Never! My life is over!

Voice of God: Do you really think your life is over, John?

Football Player: Of course I do! My whole life was football and now I won't even be able to play a backyard game of it with my own kids. It stinks!

Voice of God: Your life is far from over, John. Why it's just beginning.

Football Player: Just beginning? Not hardly!

Voice of God: I never planned for any man's worth to come from what he could do or accomplish on the outside. Your worth comes from within — from what *I* have made you.

Football Player: From within? There's nothing within me that can even come close to the way I could handle a football.

Voice of God: Right now you might not think so. But I know better. My Son's death has made all my children worthy, and I have blessed them with every gift they need for this life. My life is in you, John, and even if you never pick up a football again, you are of inestimable worth.

Football Player: Well, if that's true, you're gonna have to show me, because right now I just can't see it!

Voice of God: John, I only ask you to have faith that what I am telling you is true. Trust me, John. You are a whole person when I live in you, and I can do much with your life. There are so many more joys you can experience with me that you never even dreamed about when you were playing football. Allow me to show them to you.

Football Player: Oh, God, I want to believe you! Please lift me up out of this pit!

Voice of God: I will, John. We are embarking on a new journey — together! Call to me and I will answer you, and I will tell you great and mighty things which you do not know.[7]

Songs: "Hark! The Herald Angels Sing"
"As Each Happy Christmas"

Scene IX — *The Questioning Child*

Voice of God: There is a little boy standing behind the Christmas tree.

Angel 1: Yes, I see him, Lord.

Angel 2: He looks frightened.

Voice of God: He is frightened and unsure. He wants to come to my manger. Gently prod him over. *(Angels lead the child to the manger)*

Boy: *(Stands quietly in front of the manger in cautious wonder)* Who is this baby? I see this scene every Christmas but no one has ever told me what it means. *(Calls to someone passing by)* Hey, who is this baby? *(People walk by looking at him, but hurry on without responding. Boy shakes his head)* Won't anyone tell me what this is all about? Somehow I think it's very special, but no one will tell me.

Voice of God: And how can they believe in the one of whom they have not heard?[8] Let the little children come to me, and do not hinder them, for the kingdom of God belongs to such as these.[9]

Boy: *(Looking around to those passing by)* Hey! What's this all about? Who is this baby?

Passerby: Why, that's Jesus. Haven't you ever heard of Jesus?

Boy: Well, I've heard people say Jesus, but only when they're mad.

Passerby: *(Slowly kneels next to boy)* Well, let me tell you, son. There are a lot of people who don't know who Jesus really is, except as a curse word. But he really is someone special.

Boy: Why is he special? Is he still a baby? What does he ...

Passerby: My, my. You really don't know anything about him, do you? Well, let me see. How shall I begin ... *(Passerby and boy pretend to be in conversation together as the organ or piano softly plays "What Child is This?" and as God speaks.)*

Voice of God: Oh, yes! Heed my call to spread my Word. So many have not heard the news of my love. Tell them about how I came for them and died for them. Tell them how much I love them and will make their lives new and fulfilled. Tell them how I am with them wherever they go and that someday I will take them home to heaven to live with me forever. Tell them ... tell them ... Yes! ... Tell them!

Song: "What Child is This?"

Scene X — *Mr. Good Man*

Voice of God: Mr. Good Man is coming through the square. Oh, yes, he and I need to talk.

Angel 1: Mr. Good Man? Why, he is well-known and well-liked in this community.

Voice of God: Yes, he is. But I see into his heart.

Angel 2: We will lead him, Lord.

Mr. Good Man: Ah, yes. I see they put up the manger in town square. It's about time we had some good moral examples in our town.

Voice of God: Mr. Good Man. Would you kneel before me?

Mr. Good Man: Kneel and worship? Why, of course. Anything to set a good example.

Voice of God: I see you have had a very successful year, Mr. Good Man. That burn unit you established at the hospital was really needed. It will save a lot of lives.

Mr. Good Man: Oh, yes. That has been a desire of mine ever since my brother was in a bad fire years ago. I'm always trying to make improvements in the community wherever I can.

Voice of God: Your wife and children are proud of you. You are very faithful to them and love them a great deal, don't you?

Mr. Good Man: Oh, yes, Lord. Why, that's the trouble with our world today. Marriages are breaking up everywhere. Children grow up with no guidance. Why, I believe strongly in the family and good, sound morals. This world would be a much happier place if everyone would work hard at making an honest living, helping each other out, and showing more love to one another.

Voice of God: Yes, it would. *(Pauses)* Mr. Good Man, I'm so glad you paused for a moment at my manger. I've been trying to get your attention for quite some time now.

Mr. Good Man: Well, Lord, you know how busy I am. There are so many things that need to be done. By the time I go to work, give time to my wife and kids, and serve in the community ... well it seems there aren't enough hours in the day.

Voice of God: Someday it will be too late.

Mr. Good Man: Too late? Too late for what? Oh, if you mean the project I'm ...

Voice of God: No. I don't mean your latest project, Mr. Good Man. I mean your commitment to me.

Mr. Good Man: Well, Lord, someday when things settle down a little bit I'll start going to church and ...

Voice of God: Mr. Good Man — now is the time.

Mr. Good Man: Now? Well, uh ... I don't know. That's a hard step to take. I, uh ...

Voice of God: Mr. Good Man, I see your impeccable work record and your goodness to those around you — but I also see into your heart. There is a rebelliousness there toward me. You have never accepted me as Lord of your life.

Mr. Good Man: Hey! I don't get this! I'm a happy man. I don't see the need for you or ... I'm doing just fine on my own!

Voice of God: Mr. Good Man, I don't care how good you are. All men sin and fall short of the glory of God.[10] All your righteous deeds are as filthy rags to me.[11] You wouldn't be able to do even one good thing if it were not for my grace. I give life to every soul. Man is so proud of himself. He can always see the good he does. But before me he is but a helpless sinner.

Mr. Good Man: I don't understand this! I thought living a good life and helping others is what life is all about.

Voice of God: Giving your heart to me is what life is all about. I created this world and everyone in it to give glory to me. The world was not created for man, but for God.

Mr. Good Man: I don't see the point of all this. Do you go around telling people how bad they are and that they should worship the ground you walk on?

Voice of God: No, Mr. Good Man. I want you to listen very carefully. So many people see me as only a God with a big stick. Yes, I do demand perfection, because I am holy. But no one can be holy. That is why I sent my Son, Jesus. Look into the manger, Mr. Good Man. Look deeply and know that I came because I love you. Yes, you, Mr. Good Man. Even though you are proud and rebellious, I love you so much. There is no one I do not love. That is why I sent Jesus to die for the sins of everyone on the earth. And with his resurrection, the victory is yours — yours for the taking! Someday I want to take everyone to heaven to live with me eternally. It will be a life like no one has ever known or can even imagine. Yes, you do many good deeds, Mr. Good Man. But all the good deeds you do or don't do won't make me love you any more or less. I love you completely right now. Will you accept my love and forgiveness, Mr. Good Man? Will you give me your heart? *(Mr. Good Man bows his head in prayer)*

Song: "We Love Him"

Voice of God: God exalted Jesus to the highest place and gave him the name that is above every name, that at the name of Jesus every knee should bow, in heaven and on earth and under the earth, and every tongue confess that Jesus Christ is Lord, to the glory of God the Father.[12]

Song: "Every Knee Shall Bow"

(As the song is sung, all characters from the play gather around the manger and kneel.)

Benediction

Recessional Hymn: "Joy To The World"

Scripture References

1. 1 John 4:14-15
2. Philippians 2:8-11
3. Matthew 5:14a, 16
4. Ezekiel 18:30b-32
5. Psalm 46:10
6. Isaiah 41:10
7. Jeremiah 33:3
8. Romans 10:14
9. Matthew 19:14
10. Romans 3:23
11. Isaiah 64:6
12. Philippians 2:9-11

Acknowledgments Of Lesser-Known Songs

(Introduction)
"Come On, Ring Those Bells"
Text: Andrew Culverwell
Arrangement: Joseph Linn
Setting: "Christmas Comes to Lone Star Gulch"
© Copyright 1989, Lillenas Publishing Co., Kansas City, Missouri
    64141

(Scenes I and X)
"Every Knee Shall Bow"
Text and arrangement by Diane L. Gibson
© Copyright 1993

(Scene II)
"Come, Your Hearts And Voices Raising"
Text: Paul Gerhardt
Tune: German carol, fourteenth century
Setting: Lutheran Worship
© Copyright 1982, Concordia Publishing House, St. Louis, Mis-
    souri 63118-3698

(Scene III)
"We've Got A Brand New Song To Sing"
Text and Tune: Peter and Hanneke Jacobs
Setting: "Colby 4/God Uses Kids"
© Copyright 1987, Maranatha! Music, P.O. Box 31050, Laguna
    Hills, California 92654-1050

(Scene IV)
"Christmas News"
Text and Tune: Carol Greene
Setting: "Little Ones Sing Praise"
© Copyright 1989, Concordia Publishing House, St. Louis, Mis-
    souri 63118-3968

(Scene V)
"On Jordan's Bank The Baptist's Cry"
Text: Charles Coffin
Tune: adapt. Michael Praetorius
Setting: Lutheran Worship
© Copyright 1982, Concordia Publishing House St. Louis, Missouri 63118-3968

(Scene VI)
"Christmas Bells"
Text and Tune: Helen Friesen
Setting: Shining Star Publications
© Copyright 1988, A Division of Good Apple, Inc.

(Scene VII)
"When He Came"
Text: Mosie Lister
Arrangement: Joseph Linn
Setting: "Christmas Comes to Lone Star Gulch"
© Copyright 1989, Lillenas Publishing Co., Kansas City, Missouri 64141

(Scene VIII)
"As Each Happy Christmas"
Text: J. W. Hey
Translation: Mrs. H. Spaeth
Tune: John C. H. Rinck
Setting: "Little Ones Sing Praise"
© Copyright 1989, Concordia Publishing House, St. Louis, Missouri 63118-3968

(Scene X)
"We Love Him"
Text and Tune: Frank Hernandez
Setting: "Hide 'Em in Your Heart Bible Memory Melodies, Vol. 2"
© Copyright 1992, The Sparrow Corp. P.O. Box 5010, 101 Winners Circle, Brentwood, Tennessee 37024-5010